I SPOT SHAPES!

I SPOT DIAMONDS

first concepts

BY NATALIE HUMPHREY

Gareth Stevens
PUBLISHING

Diamonds are everywhere!
The sign is a diamond.

The window is
a diamond.

5

The field is a diamond.

The gem is a diamond.

The glass is a diamond.

11

The mirror is a diamond.

13

The cookie is a diamond.

14

15

The fence is a diamond.

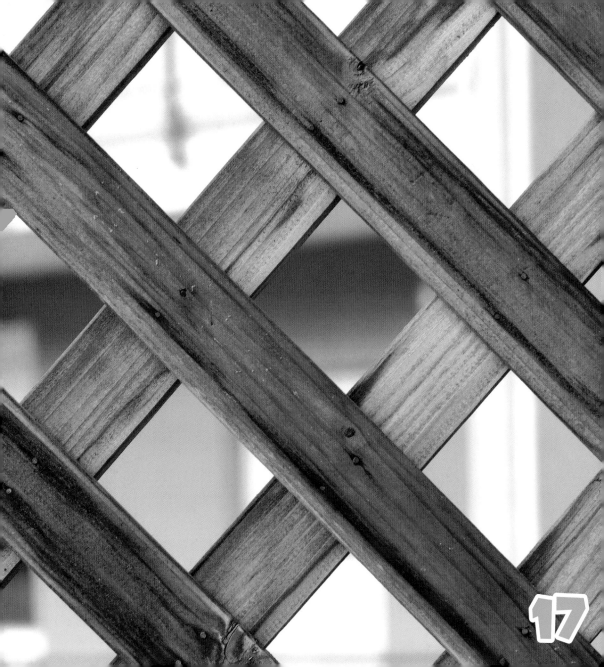

The cookie cutter is
a diamond.

The brick is a diamond.

Can you spot
the diamond?

Please visit our website, www.garethstevens.com. For a free color catalog of all our high-quality books, call toll free 1-800-542-2595 or fax 1-877-542-2596.

Library of Congress Cataloging-in-Publication Data
Names: Humphrey, Natalie, author.
Title: I spot diamonds / Natalie Humphrey.
Description: Buffalo, New York : Gareth Stevens Publishing, [2025] |
    Series: I spot shapes | Includes index.
Identifiers: LCCN 2023044262 (print) | LCCN 2023044263 (ebook) | ISBN
    9781538291719 (library binding) | ISBN 9781538291702 (paperback) | ISBN
    9781538291726 (ebook)
Subjects: LCSH: Diamonds (Shape)–Juvenile literature. | Shapes–Juvenile
    literature.
Classification: LCC QA482 .H86 2025 (print) | LCC QA482 (ebook) | DDC
    516/.154–dc23/eng/20231023
LC record available at https://lccn.loc.gov/2023044262
LC ebook record available at https://lccn.loc.gov/2023044263

Published in 2025 by
Gareth Stevens Publishing
2544 Clinton Street
West Seneca, NY 14224

Designer: Leslie Taylor
Editor: Natalie Humphrey

Photo credits: Cover Mystic Stock Photography/Shutterstock.com; p. 3 elvistudio/Shutterstock.com; p. 5 Kuznetsovadim/Shutterstock.com; p. 7 Clari Massimiliano/Shutterstock.com; p. 9 DiamondGalaxy/ Shutterstock.com; p. 11 eduard barnash/Shutterstock.com; p. 13 Harald Schmidt/Shutterstock.com; p. 15 val lawless/Shutterstock.com; p. 17 Blue Corner Studio/Shutterstock.com; p. 19 (dough) Leszek Glasner8/Shutterstock.com, (cutter) Lyutikov 713/Shutterstock.com; p. 21 Adhitya Teguh Nugraha/ Shutterstock.com; p. 23 Maranda Bankston/Shutterstock.com.

Printed in the United States of America

CPSIA compliance information: Batch #CSGS25: For further information contact Gareth Stevens, New York, New York at 1-800-542-2595.

Find us on